# Sources of Light

Louise and Richard
Spilsbury

Heinemann
raintree

Edited by Penny West
Designed by Rich Parker
Picture research by Tracy Cummins
Production by Helen McCreath
Originated by Capstone Global Library Ltd
Printed and bound in China by CTPS

19 18 17 16 15
10 9 8 7 6 5 4 3 2 1

**Library of Congress Cataloging-in-Publication Data**
Spilsbury, Louise, author.
  Sources of light / Louise Spilsbury and Richard Spilsbury.—[1st edition].
     pages cm.—(Exploring light)
  Summary: "This book looks at the different places light comes from, including natural and artificial sources. - Discover the difference between a light source and a reflective object and how you can tell which is which. - Look at our largest and most important light source - the Sun - and what happens when you take sunlight away. - Explore light technology by finding out how we use lasers and fiber optics. And much more!"—Provided by publisher.
  Includes bibliographical references and index.
  ISBN 978-1-4109-7945-2 (hb)—ISBN 978-1-4109-7950-6 (pb)—ISBN 978-1-4109-7960-5 (ebook) 1. Light sources—Juvenile literature. 2. Light—Juvenile literature.  I. Spilsbury, Richard, 1963- author. II. Title.

  QC360.S655 2016
  535—dc23                          2014039859

This book has been officially leveled by using the F&P Text Level Gradient™ Leveling System.

**Acknowledgments**
The author and publisher are grateful to the following for permission to reproduce copyright material:
Capstone Press: HL Studios, 22, Karon Dubke, 7, 8, 9, 12, 13, 16, 17, 20, 21, 24, 25, 28, 29; Getty Images: Karen Doody/ Stocktrek Image, 23;  Shutterstock: agsandrew, Design Element, Click Bestsellers, Design Element, Dennis Tokarzewski, Design Element, Dmitry Bruskov, 18, dwph, 5, focal point, 27, ID1974, Design Element, luckypic, Design Element, Maridav, 19, noppharat, 4, PandaWild, 15, Tom Reichner, 10, Valentyn Volkov, 14, Vass Zoltan, Design Element, wavebreakmedia, 11, welcomia, 6; Thinkstock: Anatoly Vartanov, 26.

Cover photo of Rudimental performing at Exit Festival in Novi Sad, Serbia, reproduced with permission of Shutterstock/ Jelena Ivanovic.

We would like to thank Catherine Jones for her invaluable help in the preparation of this book.

# Contents

Some words are shown in bold, **like this**.
You can find out what they mean by looking
in the glossary.

# Sources of Light

Light is something we use every day without thinking. We just flip on a light switch or turn on the computer and there it is. A **source** of light is something that makes or gives off light. A lamp is a source of light. The book the lamp shines on is not. Sources of light are very important. They allow us to see the world around us. Imagine what the world would be like without sources of light!

The Sun is a natural source of light that is so bright it can light up the world! The Sun is so bright it can damage your eyes very quickly, so never look directly at it.

Fireworks that light up the night sky are created by people.

A flash of lightning, the Sun, and the other stars are natural sources of light. Light sources made by people include flashlights, computers, and lamps. They use batteries and **electricity** to work. Which light sources are you using to read this book?

## Be a light detective

Investigate the light sources around you. Take a walk around your school or home and write down as many sources of light as you can. You might be surprised how many you find!

# Light on the Move

Light is useful to us because it can travel away from its **source**. Sunlight moves through space and lights up Earth. Light spreads out from a flashlight and shows our path. Light can move because it is a form of **energy**. Energy is the power that makes things work or move. Light energy travels in straight lines called **rays**. You can see this when you look at the beam of a flashlight.

We can see light traveling in straight lines in the powerful beams made by a lighthouse.

Round lightbulbs allow light rays to leave them and spread out in all directions. This maximizes the light they produce.

A flashlight shines light in one direction only, so it is easy to see that light travels in straight lines. Light from a round lightbulb can spread in all directions. The light rays travel in straight lines in different directions. That is why a light on a ceiling can light up a whole room.

## Less light!

As light gets farther away from a light source, it spreads out more. As light spreads out more, it looks less bright. That is because the light is spread over a wider area. Also, that is why the farther you get from a light source, the less bright it looks.

# Activity: The Speed of Light

Light and sound are both forms of **energy** and they can both move. Try this activity to find out if light travels faster than sound.

## What you need

- four balloons
- two friends to help
- a pin.

## What to do

**1** Inflate the four balloons and tie the ends.

**2** Ask your friends to stand in one place while you walk about 13 feet (4 meters) away from them with the balloons. Stop and pop one balloon.

**3** Your friends should all write down which came first: seeing the balloon pop or hearing the sound of the pop. They should not talk to each other about their answers.

**4** Walk so you are a further 13 feet (4 meters) away and pop a balloon again. Do this twice more until you have popped all the balloons.

**5** What did your friends notice?

## What happens?

Your friends should see the balloons pop slightly before they hear the balloons pop. This is easier to spot the farther away from the balloon they are. This proves that light energy can move faster than sound energy through air. Light is nearly a million times faster than sound. In one second, light could travel seven and a half times around the world!

# Is It a Light Source?

Light **sources** make their own light, so we can see them even when it is completely dark. That is why flashlights are so useful at night! Objects that do not make their own light are not light sources. We can only see them when **rays** of light from a light source **reflect**, or bounce, off their surface. When light hits an object, some is reflected and enters our eyes. That is how we see the object.

The Moon is not a light source. We can only see the Moon when light from the Sun reflects off it.

Shiny objects like this disco ball are not light sources, but they reflect light very well.

Mirrors and other objects reflect light so well it can look as if they are sources of light, too. That is why they look shiny. But they can only shine when light from a light source reflects off them. A shiny object will not shine in darkness.

## Reflecting light

When many rays of light hit an object, they bounce off in different directions. When reflected rays hit our eyes, we see the object they are reflecting off. In a brightly lit room, it feels as if light is all around us because the walls reflect light from a light source in all directions.

# Activity: Shine a Light

Test what happens to light **sources** with distance and less **energy**.

## What you need

- sticky tape
- a sheet of graph paper
- big books
- a small flashlight with new batteries inside
- a yardstick or tape measure
- paper and pencil.

## What to do

**1** Tape the sheet of graph paper low down on a wall, not far above the floor.

**2** Stack the books so that when you lay the flashlight on them, the flashlight is level with the graph paper.

**3** Measure 3 feet (1 meter) away from the wall and put the stack of books and flashlight here. Turn off the lights in the room and turn on the flashlight so it shines on the center of the graph paper. Measure or count the number of squares that are lit up by the flashlight. Write down the number.

**4** Measure and move the books and flashlight 4 feet (1.5 meters), 6 feet (2 meters), 8 feet (2.5 meters), and 9 feet (3 meters) away from the wall, or farther if you like. Repeat the test and count the squares the flashlight lights up each time. What do you notice?

**5** Leave the flashlight on for about an hour (or until your flashlight light looks weaker) and then do the same tests again. Repeat every hour until the flashlight batteries run out.

## What happens?

When the flashlight is moved farther away from the wall, it covers a bigger area of the graph paper. The light spreads out. As it spreads out, it gets dimmer. The flashlight batteries use energy to make the flashlight work. As the batteries run out of energy, the flashlight gives out less light.

# Heat and Light

Many light **sources** make light because they are hot. When we strike a match, **chemicals** at the tip catch fire. The wood of the match burns, and some of its heat **energy** changes into light energy. Blowing the match puts out the light, but it may still produce enough heat energy to burn. That is why we need to be careful when using matches, candles, and other flames as light sources.

Different types of energy can be changed from one form to another. Chemical energy in wood turns to heat and light energy when it burns.

In this infrared picture of a cat, the red areas are warmest and blue areas are coolest.

The melted rock or lava oozing from a volcano is not on fire but is much hotter than matches. The heat energy is so high that it makes the lava glow red. Much, much hotter objects, such as the Sun, glow white and very bright because they release even more light energy.

## Invisible light!

Animals produce heat energy. It travels in **rays** like light energy. We cannot see it because our eyes cannot detect it.

# Activity: Hot Light

Light **sources** often make heat. Test this out using desk lamps and thermometers.

## What you need

- two desk lamps: one fitted with an **incandescent** bulb, the other fitted with a **fluorescent** bulb. The bulbs should be of equivalent brightness.
- two sheets of white paper
- two digital thermometers
- an adult to help.

## What to do

 **1** Position each desk lamp over a sheet of white paper, with a distance of about 4 inches (10 centimeters) between the bulb and the paper.

 **2** Place a thermometer directly beneath each bulb, on the paper.

**3** Switch the lamps on. After five minutes, record the temperature under each lamp using the thermometer.

## Try this!

Solar collectors are devices people put on roofs. They have **liquid** inside that warms up easily in sunlight. The liquid is used to help heat water for people to use. Try making your own solar collectors by filling and sealing water bottles and leaving them outside on sunny days!

## What happens?

You should find that one bulb produces a higher temperature than the other. This is because different types of lamp produce different amounts of heat **energy** as they produce light. We say that fluorescent lamps are energy efficient because they do not waste as much energy as heat when making light.

# The Sun

Our planet's most important **source** of light is the Sun. The Sun is a gigantic ball of glowing **gas**, like all stars in the universe. Stars glow brightly and produce temperatures that are hundreds of thousands of times hotter than the hottest oven. Some of this enormous amount of **energy** travels to Earth as the **rays** of light and heat we know as sunlight.

The Sun is our closest star. It lights up and warms Earth, even when it is partly hidden behind the clouds.

Sunlight's warmth helps fruits and vegetables to ripen so they are good to eat.

Sunlight is needed for plants to grow and make their own food. Many animals survive by eating plants, and other animals eat the plant eaters. People even turn sunlight into **electricity** using devices called **solar panels**!

## A long way away

Sunlight lights and warms us even though the Sun is millions of miles from Earth. Light moves at about 186,500 miles (300,000 kilometers) per second, but it still takes eight minutes to reach us from the Sun! But that is much closer than our next-nearest star. Its light takes over four years to reach us.

# Activity: Sunny Beans

This activity shows how plants need sunlight to grow.

## What you need

- four paper towel sheets
- a spray bottle filled with water
- two glass jars with lids
- two bean seeds
- aluminum foil.

## What to do

**1** Fold up two sheets of paper towel, moisten, and place in one jar. Repeat for the second jar.

**2** Put one bean down the side of the jar, so it is between the paper towels and the glass (so you can see it from the side of the jar).

**3** Put the lids on the jars ar wrap one completely in fo so the inside of it is dark.

bean grown
in the light

bean grown
in the dark

Leave both jars on a
light, warm windowsill
for 10 days, opening each
to spray the seeds with
water every few days.

## Try this

Once the seedling has
emerged from the seed,
place its jar at one end of a
shoe box sealed shut.
Carefully cut a small hole
in the lid at the opposite
end. Did your plant grow
toward the light?

## What happens?

Both seeds **germinate**, or grow, proving that
sunlight is not needed for this first stage in a
plant's life. But the main shoot of the plant kept in
the dark is less green and more spindly. Its leaves
are withered and pale. Light is needed for the
young plant to grow the green leaves it can use to
make food and thrive.

# Cool Lights

Not all light **sources** get hot to give off light. When you crack a glowstick, tubes inside containing different **chemicals** break so they start to mix together. This produces a chemical change that releases some **energy** as light and very little as heat energy. The stick stops glowing once all the chemicals are mixed and used up.

We can see objects such as some watch faces in the dark at night or under bed covers because energy from light is continuing to make special chemicals glow.

Caribbean reef squid can change their color patterns to communicate with other squid. They are even able to create one pattern on their left side to send one message, and a different one on their right!

Some animals can give off light in a similar way to glowsticks. Male fireflies use patterns of light flashes to tell female fireflies where they are. They take in air and mix it with a substance inside their body to make a light with almost no heat at all.

## Light to catch prey

Female anglerfish have a rod above their mouth tipped with a light source. Shrimp and other small creatures are attracted to the light, and the anglerfish gulps them up when they get close enough!

# Activity: Light from Sugar

Some **materials** become light **sources** when they are crushed, torn, or rubbed. One of these is a common, sweet kitchen ingredient.

## Warning!

Do this with an adult and be gentle so you do not break the glass or the plate.

## What you need

- white sugar cubes
- a plate
- a flat-bottomed and strong drinking glass.

## What to do

**1** Place a sugar cube on the plate.

**2** Push firmly but gently down on the sugar cubes, rocking the glass. Do not bang the glass on the plate. Repeat several times so you get used to crushing the sugar cubes carefully. You can leave all the crushed sugar on the plate.

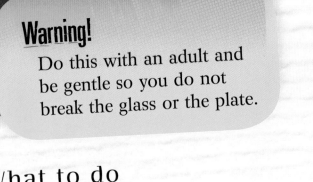

## Try this

Some sticky substances can also become light sources when ripped in the dark!

- Seal and then rip open a self-sealing envelope.
- Fold a length of duct tape in half so it is stuck to itself, leaving each end folded over by half an inch (1 cm). Then rip apart!

**3** Now crush new sugar cubes using this method in a very dark room with all the lights turned off. What do you see?

## What happens?

You should see flashes of glowing blue light from the crushed sugar cubes because some **energy** from crushing the sugar changes into light energy. This light is so weak that it can only be seen faintly in a very dark room and not in a lit room.

# Using Light Sources

People have made special light **sources** to use in different ways. **Lasers** are machines that make narrow, powerful beams of light. The beams can be used to play DVDs and for cutting things accurately and carefully. In factories, lasers cut through tough metals or hundreds of layers of fabric at once!

Laser beams do not spread out like ordinary light. They can be focused in one direction to do a job.

## Bar codes

Bar codes are the strips of lines you see on store labels. A bar code reader uses a laser beam to scan bar codes. It detects the line widths and spacing on the bar code to identify the item and its price.

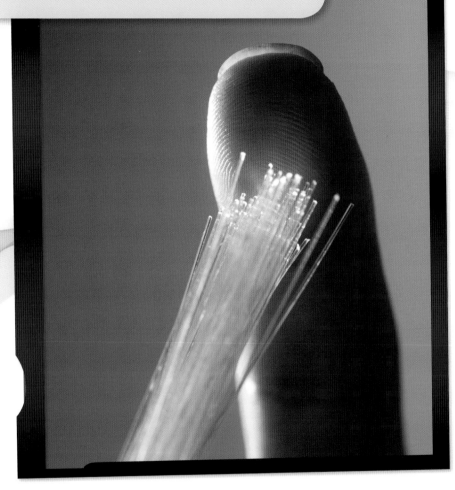

A bundle of optical fibers as thin as a little finger can carry tens of thousands of light messages at once. That is far more information than a normal cable the thickness of your arm could carry!

People also use light sources to send information. For example, phone messages can be changed into patterns of light flashes and sent through very long **optical fibers**. Optical fibers are thin, flexible, and transparent glass rods. The light flashes move through the rods without shining out from the sides.

# Activity: Pouring Light

Try sending a light message without **optical fibers**, using a bottle of water and a flashlight!

## What you need

- a clear plastic bottle, such as a medium water or soda bottle
- aluminum foil
- sticky tape
- a dark room with a sink, such as a bathroom
- a flashlight.

## What to do

**1** Wrap the bottle completely in foil, but leave the base bare. Use sticky tape to secure the foil.

**2** Fill the bottle almost to the top with water. Then switch on your flashlight and turn off the lights.

**3** Shine the flashlight through the bare base of the bottle as you hold the bottle on its side, and start to gently and slowly pour the water into a sink. Hold the bottle as high as you can without splashing water on the floor! Keep the flashlight close to the base of the bottle at all times.

## What happens?

Hopefully you will see a spot of bright light where the water hits the sink. This is because almost all of the light from the flashlight is **reflected** every time it hits the edge of the stream of water. Therefore, the light moves from the **source** along the path of the water as it pours.

# Glossary

**chemical** distinct or particular substance that is the same all the way through. Some chemicals are natural, such as water. Other chemicals are made by people, such as the chlorine used in swimming pools.

**electricity** type of energy we usually use to make machines work

**energy** the power that makes things work or move

**fluorescent** something that makes light when electricity flows through a tube filled with a type of gas

**gas** thing that has no shape or size of its own. Gases, such as the air around us, can spread out in all directions and change shape to fit any space.

**germinate** to start to grow. Plant seeds germinate.

**incandescent** giving out light energy because it is heated

**laser** narrow, very powerful beam of light used in DVDs, CDs, and to cut through things

**liquid** thing that is runny and cannot be held easily in your hands, such as water, milk, or juice

**material** something we use or make other things from, such as wood, rubber, or plastic

**optical fiber** thin rod of high-quality glass that carries messages coded in light signals

**ray** narrow line or beam of light

**reflect** to bounce back off a surface

**solar panel** panel that absorbs the Sun's rays and uses their energy to make electricity or heat

**source** person or thing that starts something. A light source gives off light.

# Find Out More

## Books

Ballard, Carol. *Exploring Light* (How Does Science Work?). New York: PowerKids, 2008.

Claybourne, Anna. *Glaring Light and Other Eye-Burning Rays* (Disgusting and Dreadful Science). New York: Crabtree, 2013.

Hewitt, Sally. *Light* (Amazing Science). New York: Crabtree, 2008.

Riley, Peter. *Light* (The Real Scientist Investigates). N. Mankato, Minn.: Sea-to-Sea, 2011.

## Web sites

Facthound offers a safe, fun way to find Internet sites related to this book. All of the sites on Facthound have been researched by our staff.

Here's all you do:

Visit www.facthound.com

Type in this code: 9781410979452

# Index